THE RUBY COI

A PROGRAMMER'S GUIDE TO THE RUBY UNIVERSE

OLIVER LUCAS JR

1

TABLE OF CONTENTS

Preface

Embarking on Your Ruby Journey

Welcome to *The Ruby Codex: A Programmer's Guide to the Ruby Universe*. This book is a comprehensive exploration of the Ruby programming language, designed to guide you from novice to expert.

Ruby, with its elegant syntax and powerful features, has captured the hearts of developers worldwide. Its emphasis on programmer happiness and productivity makes it an ideal language for both beginners and seasoned programmers.

What This Book Offers

A Solid Foundation: This book provides a solid foundation in Ruby's core concepts, including variables, data types, control flow, and object-oriented programming.

Practical Applications: You'll learn how to apply Ruby to real-world problems, such as web development, data processing, and system administration.

Advanced Techniques: Explore advanced topics like metaprogramming, concurrency, and functional programming.

Best Practices: Gain insights into best practices for writing clean, efficient, and maintainable Ruby code.

Who This Book Is For

This book is for anyone who wants to learn Ruby, regardless of their programming experience. Whether you're a complete beginner or an experienced programmer looking to add Ruby to your toolkit, you'll find valuable information within these pages.

Let's Begin

Chapter 1

Embarking on the Ruby Journey

1.1 Understanding Ruby's Philosophy: Exploring the Elegance and Simplicity of Ruby

Introduction

Ruby, a dynamic, interpreted, high-level programming language, has captured the hearts of developers worldwide due to its elegant syntax and focus on programmer happiness.[1] Created by Yukihiro "Matz" Matsumoto in the mid-1990s, Ruby was designed with the intention of making programming more enjoyable and productive.[2]

The Philosophy of Ruby

Ruby's design philosophy centers around the idea that programming should be a pleasurable experience.[3] Matz often emphasizes the importance of "programmer happiness," and this principle is evident in every aspect of the language.[4]Ruby's syntax is designed to be intuitive and readable, often resembling natural language.[5] This emphasis on readability and simplicity makes it easier to learn and maintain Ruby code.[6]

Key principles of Ruby's philosophy

Simplicity: Ruby's syntax is designed to be concise and easy to understand.[7] It avoids unnecessary complexity and focuses on providing a clear and straightforward way to express ideas.[8]

Expressiveness: Ruby allows developers to write code that is both powerful and elegant.[9] Its rich set of features and expressive syntax enables you to convey complex ideas in a concise and readable manner.[10]

Productivity: Ruby's focus on simplicity and expressiveness leads to increased productivity.[11] You can write more code in less time, and the code you write is more likely to be correct and maintainable.

Community: The Ruby community is known for its friendliness and helpfulness.[12] This supportive community fosters collaboration and knowledge sharing, making it easier to learn and use Ruby.[13]

Ruby's Syntax: Simple and Readable

One of the most striking features of Ruby is its elegant and readable syntax.[14] Here's a simple example of a Ruby program that prints "Hello, world!":

```
Ruby
puts "Hello, world!"
```

As you can see, Ruby's syntax is very close to natural language, making it easy to read and understand.[15]

Object-Oriented Programming in Ruby

Ruby is a pure object-oriented language, which means that everything in Ruby is an object, including numbers, strings, and even[16] classes themselves.[17] This object-oriented paradigm promotes modularity, reusability, and code organization.[18]

The Power of Ruby: Blocks, Procs, and Lambdas

Ruby's powerful functional programming features, such as blocks, procs, and lambdas, allow you to write concise and expressive code.[19] These features enable you to pass code blocks as arguments to methods, making your code more flexible and reusable.[20]

Ruby on Rails: A Testament to Ruby's Versatility

Ruby on Rails, a popular web application framework built on Ruby, is a testament to the language's versatility and power.[21] Rails provides a comprehensive set of tools and conventions for building web applications quickly and efficiently.[22]

Conclusion

Ruby's elegant syntax, powerful features, and active community make it a compelling choice for developers of all levels.[23] By understanding Ruby's philosophy and embracing its core principles, you can write more efficient, maintainable, and enjoyable code.

1.2   Writing Your First Ruby Program: A Gentle Introduction to Ruby Syntax

Setting Up Your Ruby Environment

1. Installation:

Windows: Download the Ruby installer from the official Ruby website (https://www.ruby-lang.org/en/) and follow the installation instructions.

macOS: Ruby often comes pre-installed on macOS. You can check the version by opening the Terminal and typing `ruby -v`. If not installed, you can use Homebrew to install it: `brew install ruby`.

Linux: Use your package manager to install Ruby. For example, on Ubuntu/Debian, you can use `sudo apt install ruby-full`.

2. Text Editor:

Choose a text editor or IDE that supports syntax highlighting for Ruby. Popular options include:

Visual Studio Code

Sublime Text

Atom

Vim

Emacs

Your First Ruby Program: Hello, World!

Create a New File:

Open your chosen text editor and create a new file.

Save the file with a `.rb` extension (e.g., `hello.rb`).

Write the Code:

Ruby
puts "Hello, world!

Run the Program:
Open your terminal or command prompt.
Navigate to the directory where you saved the `hello.rb` file.
Type the following command and press Enter:
Bash
ruby hello.rb

This will execute the Ruby script, and you should see the output "Hello, world!" printed to the console.

Understanding the Code

`puts`: This is a method in Ruby that prints a string to the console.

`"Hello, world!"`: This is a string literal, representing the text to be printed.

Basic Ruby Syntax

Comments:

Ruby

```ruby
# This is a single-line comment
=begin
This is a
multi-line comment
=end
```

Variables:
Ruby
```ruby
name = "Alice"
age = 30
```

Numbers:
Ruby
integer_number = 42
floating_point_number = 3.14
Strings:
Ruby
single_quoted_string = 'Hello'
double_quoted_string = "World"
Boolean Values:

Ruby
true
false

Experimenting Further

Print Multiple Lines:

Ruby

puts "Line 1"
puts "Line 2"
Arithmetic Operations:
Ruby
result = 5 + 3
puts result
String Concatenation:

Ruby
first_name = "John"
last_name = "Doe"
full_name = first_name + " " + last_name
puts full_name

By understanding these basic concepts, you're well on your way to mastering Ruby programming. Keep practicing and exploring the language's rich features.

Chapter 2

Ruby Fundamentals

2.1 Variables and Data Types in Ruby

Variables

A variable in Ruby is a named storage location that holds a value. You can think of it as a container that can store different types of data. To declare a variable, you simply assign a value to it using the = operator.

Ruby
```
name = "Alice"
age = 30
```

Data Types

Ruby is a dynamically typed language, which means you don't need to explicitly declare the data type of a variable. The interpreter[1] automatically determines the data type based on the value assigned to[2] it.

Here are some of the common data types in Ruby:

1. Numbers

Integers: Whole numbers without decimal points.

Ruby
```
integer_number = 42
```
Floating-Point Numbers: Numbers with decimal points.
Ruby

floating_point_number = 3.14

2. Strings

Sequences of characters enclosed in single or double quotes.

```Ruby
single_quoted_string = 'Hello'
double_quoted_string = "World"
```

3. Booleans

Represents truth values, either true or false.

```Ruby
is_true = true
is_false = false
```

4. Nil

Represents the absence of a value.

```Ruby
nothing = nil
```

5. Symbols

Immutable objects often used as identifiers or keys in hashes.

```Ruby
symbol = :ruby
```

Working with Data Types

Ruby provides various methods and operators to work with different data types:

Numbers

Arithmetic Operators: +, -, *, /, %

Comparison Operators: ==, !=, <, >, <=, >=

Mathematical Functions: Math.sqrt, Math.sin, Math.cos, etc.

```Ruby
result = 5 + 3
puts result

is_equal = 5 == 3
puts is_equal
```

Strings

Concatenation: + operator

Interpolation: #{} syntax

String Methods: length, upcase, downcase, reverse, etc.

```Ruby
first_name = "John"
last_name = "Doe"
full_name = first_name + " " + last_name
puts full_name

greeting = "Hello, #{name}!"
puts greeting
```

Booleans

Logical Operators: &&, | |, !

Ruby
is_adult = age >= 18
is_eligible = is_adult && has_license

By understanding these fundamental data types and their operations, you can build more complex and sophisticated Ruby programs.

2.2 Operators and Expressions in Ruby

Operators are special symbols that perform specific operations on values, known as operands. **Expressions** are combinations of values, variables, and operators that evaluate to a single value.

Arithmetic Operators

These operators perform basic arithmetic operations:

Addition: +

Subtraction: −

Multiplication: *

Division: /

Modulo[1] (Remainder): %

Exponentiation: **

```ruby
Ruby
result = 10 + 5
puts result  # Output: 15

remainder = 15 % 4
puts remainder  # Output: 3

power = 2 ** 3
puts power  # Output: 8
```

Comparison Operators

These operators compare values and return a boolean result (true or false):

Equal to: ==

Not Equal to: !=

Greater Than: >

Less Than: <

Greater Than or Equal To: >=

Less Than or Equal To:[2] <=

```ruby
Ruby
is_equal = 5 == 5
puts is_equal  # Output: true

is_greater = 10 > 7
puts is_greater  # Output: true
```

Logical Operators

These operators combine boolean expressions:

Logical AND: && (Both operands must be true)

Logical OR: | | (At least one operand must be true)

Logical NOT: ! (Reverses the boolean value)

```ruby
Ruby
is_adult = age >= 18
has_license = true

is_eligible_to_drive = is_adult && has_license
puts is_eligible_to_drive  # Output: true (if age >= 18)
```

Assignment Operators

These operators assign values to variables:

Simple Assignment: =

Addition Assignment: +=

Subtraction Assignment: -=

Multiplication Assignment: *=

Division Assignment: /=

Modulo Assignment: %=

```ruby
Ruby
x = 10
x += 5  # Equivalent to x = x + 5
```

```
puts x  # Output: 15
```

By understanding these operators and expressions, you can build complex calculations and logical conditions in your Ruby programs.

2.3 Control Flow Statements in Ruby

Control flow statements allow you to control the execution flow of your Ruby programs. They help you make decisions and repeat code blocks based on certain conditions.

Conditional Statements

1. if Statement

Executes a block of code only if a given condition is true.

```
Ruby
age = 25

if age >= 18
  puts "You are an adult."
end
```

2. if-else Statement

Executes one block of code if the condition is true, and another if it's false.

```
Ruby
age = 15

if age >= 18
  puts "You are an adult."
```

```ruby
else
  puts "You are a minor."
end
```

3. if-elsif-else Statement

Allows you to check multiple conditions and execute different code blocks based on the first true condition.

Ruby
```ruby
score = 85

if score >= 90
  puts "Excellent!"
elsif score >= 80
  puts "Very Good!"
elsif score >= 70
  puts "Good"
else
  puts "Needs Improvement"
end
```

Looping Statements

1. while Loop

Repeats a block of code as long as a given condition is true.

Ruby
```ruby
count = 0

while count < 5
  puts "Count: #{count}"
  count += 1
end
```

2. until Loop

Repeats a block of code until a given condition becomes true.

```ruby
Ruby
count = 0

until count == 5
  puts "Count: #{count}"
  count += 1
end
```

3. for Loop

Iterates over a range of values or elements in an array.

```ruby
Ruby
for i in 1..5
  puts i
end

fruits = ["apple", "banana", "cherry"]
for fruit in fruits
  puts fruit
end
```

4. each Loop

Iterates over each element in an array or hash.

```ruby
Ruby
fruits = ["apple", "banana", "cherry"]
fruits.each do |fruit|
```

```
    puts fruit
end
```

By effectively using control flow statements, you can create more dynamic and responsive Ruby programs.

2.3 Control Flow Statements in Ruby

Control flow statements allow you to control the execution flow of your Ruby programs. They help you make decisions and repeat code blocks based on certain conditions.

Conditional Statements

1. if Statement

Executes a block of code only if a given condition is true.

```
Ruby
age = 25

if age >= 18
  puts "You are an adult."
end
```

2. if-else Statement

Executes one block of code if the condition is true, and another if it's false.

```
Ruby
age = 15

if age >= 18
  puts "You are an adult."
```

```
else
  puts "You are a minor."
end
```

3. if-elsif-else Statement

Allows you to check multiple conditions and execute different code blocks based on the first true condition.

Ruby
```
score = 85

if score >= 90
  puts "Excellent!"
elsif score >= 80
  puts "Very Good!"
elsif score >= 70
  puts "Good"
else
  puts "Needs Improvement"
end
```

Looping Statements

1. while Loop

Repeats a block of code as long as a given condition is true.

Ruby
```
count = 0

while count < 5
  puts "Count: #{count}"
  count += 1
end
```

2. until Loop

Repeats a block of code until a given condition becomes true.

```ruby
Ruby
count = 0

until count == 5
  puts "Count: #{count}"
  count += 1
end
```

3. for Loop

Iterates over a range of values or elements in an array.

```ruby
Ruby
for i in 1..5
  puts i
end

fruits = ["apple", "banana", "cherry"]
for fruit in fruits
  puts fruit
end
```

4. each Loop

Iterates over each element in an array or hash.

```ruby
Ruby
fruits = ["apple", "banana", "cherry"]
fruits.each do |fruit|
```

```
  puts fruit
end
```

By effectively using control flow statements, you can create more dynamic and responsive Ruby programs.

Chapter 3

Methods and Classes

3.1 Defining Methods in Ruby

Methods are blocks of code that perform specific tasks. They help you organize your code, make it reusable, and improve readability.

Basic Syntax:

```ruby
Ruby
def method_name
  # Code to be executed
end
```

Example:

```ruby
Ruby
def greet
  puts "Hello, world!"
end

greet  # Call the method
```

Methods with Parameters:

You can pass arguments to a method to make it more flexible.

```ruby
Ruby
def greet_name(name)
  puts "Hello, #{name}!"
end
```

```ruby
greet_name("Alice")
```

Methods with Return Values:

You can use the `return` keyword to specify the value that a method should return.

Ruby
```ruby
def square(number)
  return number * number
end

result = square(5)
puts result  # Output: 25
```

Implicit Return:

Ruby implicitly returns the value of the last expression in a method.

Ruby
```ruby
def square(number)
  number * number
end
```

Method Chaining:

You can chain method calls on objects to create more concise code.

Ruby
```ruby
"Hello, world!".upcase.reverse
```

Common Methods:

`puts`: Prints a string to the console.

`print`: Prints a string to the console without a newline.

`gets`: Reads a line of input from the user.

`to_i`: Converts a string to an integer.

`to_f`: Converts a string to a floating-point number.

By effectively using methods, you can break down complex problems into smaller, more manageable functions, making your code more modular and easier to maintain.

3.2 Object-Oriented Programming (OOP) Concepts in Ruby

Object-Oriented Programming (OOP) is a programming paradigm that organizes software design around data, or objects, rather than functions and[1] logic. Ruby is a pure object-oriented language, meaning everything in Ruby is an object.

Core OOP Concepts in Ruby

1. Classes

A class is a blueprint for creating objects. It defines the properties (attributes) and behaviors (methods) that objects of that class will[2] have.

Ruby
```
class Dog
  def initialize(name, breed)
    @name = name
```

```ruby
    @breed = breed
  end

  def bark
    puts "#{@name} barks!"
  end
end
```

2. Objects

An object is an instance of a class. It has its own set of properties and can perform the actions defined by the class.

```ruby
Ruby
my_dog = Dog.new("Buddy", "Golden Retriever")
my_dog.bark  # Output: Buddy barks!
```

3. Inheritance

Inheritance allows you to create new classes based on existing ones. The new class (child class or subclass) inherits the properties and methods of the parent class (superclass).

```ruby
Ruby
class GoldenRetriever < Dog
  def fetch
    puts "#{@name} fetches!"
  end
end

my_golden = GoldenRetriever.new("Max", "Golden Retriever")
my_golden.bark  # Output: Max barks!
my_golden.fetch  # Output: Max fetches!
```

Additional OOP Concepts

1. Encapsulation

Encapsulation is the bundling of data (attributes) and methods that operate on that data within a single unit[3] (class). This helps protect the internal state of an object and prevents unintended modifications.

2. Polymorphism

Polymorphism allows objects of different classes to be treated as if they were objects of the same class. This is often achieved through[4] method overriding and method overloading.

3. Modules and Mixins

Modules are a way to group methods and constants. They can be included in classes to provide additional functionality. Mixins are a way to share code between unrelated classes.

By understanding these core OOP concepts, you can write more organized, reusable, and maintainable Ruby code.

3.3 Modules and Mixins in Ruby

Modules

Modules are a way to group methods and constants. They are used to organize code and share functionality between different classes. Modules can be included in other classes using the `include` keyword.

Creating a Module:

Ruby
module Swimmable

```
  def swim
    puts "I can swim!"
  end
end
```

Including a Module:

```
Ruby
class Duck
  include Swimmable
end

duck = Duck.new
duck.swim  # Output: I can swim!
```

Mixins

Mixins are a way to share code between unrelated classes. They are similar to modules, but they are often used to add specific behaviors to classes that don't share a common ancestor.

Creating a Mixin Module:

```
Ruby
module Flyable
  def fly
    puts "I can fly!"
  end
end
```

Including a Mixin:

```
Ruby
class Bird
```

```ruby
  include Flyable
end

class Airplane
  include Flyable
end

bird = Bird.new
bird.fly  # Output: I can fly!

plane = Airplane.new
plane.fly  # Output: I can fly!
```

Key Differences Between Modules and Mixins:

Feature	Modules	Mixins
Inheritance	No inheritance	No inheritance
Namespace	Creates a namespace	Doesn't create a namespace
Purpose	Organizing code, sharing functionality	Adding specific behaviors to unrelated classes

Best Practices

Use modules to organize code and share functionality between related classes.

Use mixins to add specific behaviors to unrelated classes.

Avoid overusing mixins, as they can make code more complex to understand and maintain.

Consider using composition over inheritance when possible.

By understanding modules and mixins, you can write more modular, reusable, and well-organized Ruby code.

Chapter 4

Working with Data Structures

4.1 Arrays and Hashes in Ruby

Arrays

An array is an ordered collection of elements. It's like a list where each element has a specific index.

Creating an Array:

```
Ruby
fruits = ["apple", "banana", "cherry"]
```

Accessing Elements:

```
Ruby
first_fruit = fruits[0]  # Accessing the first element
last_fruit = fruits[-1]  # Accessing the last element
```

Iterating Over an Array:

```
Ruby
fruits.each do |fruit|
  puts fruit
end
```

Adding Elements:

```
Ruby
fruits << "orange"  # Add an element to the end
```

```ruby
fruits.unshift("grape")  # Add an element to the beginning
```

Removing Elements:

Ruby
```ruby
fruits.pop  # Remove the last element
fruits.shift  # Remove the first element
```

Hashes

A hash is an unordered collection of key-value pairs. It's like a dictionary where each key maps to a specific value.

Creating a Hash:

Ruby
```ruby
person = {
  name: "Alice",
  age: 30,
  city: "New York"
}
```

Accessing Values:

Ruby
```ruby
name = person[:name]
age = person["age"]
```

Adding Key-Value Pairs:

Ruby
```ruby
person[:occupation] = "Engineer"
```

Iterating Over a Hash:

```ruby
Ruby
person.each do |key, value|
  puts "#{key}: #{value}"
end
```

Key Points:

Arrays are ordered collections, while hashes are unordered.

Arrays use integer indices to access elements.

Hashes use keys to access values.

Both arrays and hashes are mutable, meaning you can modify their contents after creation.

By understanding arrays and hashes, you can effectively store and organize data in your Ruby programs.

4.2 Strings and Regular Expressions in Ruby

Strings

Strings are sequences of characters enclosed in single or double quotes. Ruby provides a rich set of methods for manipulating strings.

Creating Strings:

```ruby
Ruby
single_quoted_string = 'Hello, world!'
double_quoted_string = "Hello, \"world\"!"
```

Accessing Characters:

Ruby
```
first_char = "Hello"[0]  # Access the first character
last_char = "Hello"[-1]  # Access the last character
```

String Methods:

`length`: Returns the length of the string.

`upcase`: Converts the string to uppercase.

`downcase`: Converts the string to lowercase.

`capitalize`: Capitalizes the first letter of the string.

`reverse`: Reverses the characters in the string.

`split`: Splits the string into an array of substrings based on a delimiter.

`join`: Joins the elements of an array into a string.

Ruby
```
string = "Hello, world!"
length = string.length  # 13
uppercase_string = string.upcase  # "HELLO, WORLD!"
words = string.split(" ")  # ["Hello,", "world!"]
```

Regular Expressions

Regular expressions are patterns used to match specific sequences of characters within a string. Ruby's `Regexp` class provides powerful tools for working with regular expressions.

Creating a Regular Expression:

Ruby
```
regex = /hello/  # Matches the word "hello"
```

Matching a String:

Ruby
```
string = "Hello, world!"
match = string =~ regex  # Returns the starting index of the match (0)
```

Extracting Matches:

Ruby
```
email_regex = /\w+@\w+\.\w+/
email_string = "My email is john.doe@example.com"
match_data = email_regex.match(email_string)
email = match_data[0]  # "john.doe@example.com"
```

Common Regular Expression Metacharacters:

. Matches any single character except a newline.

^ Matches the beginning of a string.

$ Matches the end of a string.

* Matches zero or more repetitions of the preceding element.

+ Matches one or more repetitions of the preceding element.

? Matches zero or one repetition of the preceding element.[1]

[ ] Matches any character within the brackets.

\d Matches a digit.

\w Matches a word character (alphanumeric or underscore).

\s Matches a whitespace character.

By mastering strings and regular expressions, you can effectively manipulate text and perform complex text processing tasks in Ruby.

4.3 Numbers and Mathematical Operations in Ruby

Ruby supports various numerical data types:

Integers: Whole numbers like 10, -5, 0.

Floating-Point Numbers: Numbers with decimal points like 3.14, -2.5.

Basic Arithmetic Operations

You can perform basic arithmetic operations using the standard operators:

Addition: +

Subtraction: -

Multiplication: *

Division: /

Modulo (Remainder): %

Exponentiation: **

```ruby
Ruby
result = 10 + 5
puts result  # Output: 15

remainder = 15 % 4
puts remainder  # Output: 3

power = 2 ** 3
puts power  # Output: 8
```

Mathematical Functions

Ruby provides a `Math` module that includes many mathematical functions:

```ruby
Ruby
# Square root
sqrt = Math.sqrt(16)
puts sqrt  # Output: 4.0

# Trigonometric functions
sin_value = Math.sin(Math::PI / 2)
puts sin_value  # Output: 1.0

# Exponential function
exp_value = Math.exp(2)
puts exp_value  # Output: 7.38905609893065
```

Number Conversion

You can convert numbers between different data types:

```ruby
Ruby
integer_number = 10
float_number = integer_number.to_f  # Convert to float

float_number = 3.14
integer_number = float_number.to_i  # Convert to integer
```

Number Formatting

You can format numbers using string interpolation and formatting methods:

```ruby
Ruby
price = 1234.56
formatted_price = "$%.2f" % price
puts formatted_price  # Output: $1234.56
```

By understanding these basic concepts and using the provided methods and functions, you can perform a wide range of numerical calculations in your Ruby programs.

Chapter 5

Input/Output Operations

5.1 Reading and Writing Files in Ruby

Ruby provides a straightforward way to interact with the file system. Here's how you can read from and write to files:

Reading Files

1. Reading the Entire File:

```ruby
Ruby
file = File.open("file.txt", "r")
contents = file.read
file.close

puts contents
```

2. Reading Line by Line:

```ruby
Ruby
File.open("file.txt", "r") do |file|
  file.each_line do |line|
    puts line
  end
end
```

Writing Files

1. Writing to a New File:

Ruby
```ruby
File.open("new_file.txt", "w") do |file|
  file.write("Hello, world!")
end
```

2. Appending to an Existing File:

Ruby
```ruby
File.open("log.txt", "a") do |file|
  file.write("This is a new line.\n")
end
```

Key Points:

File Modes:

r: Read-only mode

w: Write-only mode (creates a new file or truncates an existing one)

a: Append mode (appends to the end of an existing file or creates a new one)

r+: Read-write mode

File Handles:

It's good practice to close files after use to release system resources.

The File.open method with a block automatically closes the file when the block ends.

Error Handling:

Use `begin-rescue` blocks to handle potential exceptions like file not found or permission errors.

Example with Error Handling:

```ruby
Ruby
begin
  File.open("data.txt", "r") do |file|
    contents = file.read
    puts contents
  end
rescue Errno::ENOENT => e
  puts "File not found: #{e.message}"
end
```

By understanding these concepts and using the provided methods, you can effectively interact with the file system in your Ruby programs.

5.2 Command-Line Arguments in Ruby

Command-line arguments allow you to pass information to your Ruby script when you execute it from the terminal. This is useful for customizing the script's behavior without modifying the code itself.

Accessing Command-Line Arguments

Ruby provides the ARGV global variable to access command-line arguments. It's an array that contains the arguments passed to the script.

```ruby
Ruby
# Assuming the script is run as: ruby script.rb Alice 30
puts ARGV[0]  # Output: Alice
puts ARGV[1]  # Output: 30
```

Parsing Command-Line Arguments

For more complex scenarios, you can use the `OptionParser` library to parse command-line options and arguments.

```ruby
Ruby
require 'optparse'

options = {}
OptionParser.new do |opts|
  opts.on("-n NAME", "--name NAME", "Your name") do |name|
    options[:name] = name
  end

  opts.on("-a AGE", "--age AGE", "Your age") do |age|
    options[:age] = age.to_i
  end
end.parse!

puts "Name: #{options[:name]}"
puts "Age: #{options[:age]}"
```

Key Points:

The first element of ARGV is the script name itself.

Use ARGV.length to get the number of arguments passed.

The `OptionParser` library provides a flexible way to parse complex command-line options.

Always validate and sanitize user input to prevent security vulnerabilities.

By understanding command-line arguments, you can create more flexible and customizable Ruby scripts.

5.3 Standard Input and Output in Ruby

Standard Input (STDIN)

Standard input refers to the default input stream, typically the keyboard. In Ruby, you can read input from the user using the `gets` method.

Ruby
```
print "Enter your name: "
name = gets.chomp  # Remove the trailing newline character

puts "Hello, #{name}!"
```

Standard Output (STDOUT)

Standard output refers to the default output stream, typically the console. You can write output to the console using the `puts` and `print` methods.

Ruby
```
puts "Hello, world!"
print "This is a line of text."
```

Combining Input and Output

You can combine input and output to create interactive programs.

Ruby
```
print "Enter a number: "
number = gets.chomp.to_i

result = number * 2
puts "The result is: #{result}"
```

Key Points:

`gets`: Reads a line of input from the user.

`chomp`: Removes the trailing newline character from the input.

`puts`: Prints a string to the console followed by a newline.

`print`: Prints a string to the console without a newline.

By understanding standard input and output, you can create interactive Ruby programs that can communicate with the user.

Chapter 6

Exception Handling

6.1 Error Types and Handling in Ruby

Errors, or exceptions, are events that disrupt the normal flow of a program. Ruby provides a robust mechanism to handle errors gracefully and prevent program crashes.

Common Error Types in Ruby

SyntaxError: Occurs when the code violates Ruby's syntax rules.

NameError: Raised when a variable or method is used before being defined.

TypeError: Occurs when an operation is attempted on an object of the wrong type.

ArgumentError: Raised when a method is called with an incorrect number of arguments.

RuntimeError: A general error that can be raised for various reasons.

IOError: Raised when an I/O operation fails (e.g., file not found).

Handling Errors with `begin-rescue-end` Blocks

The `begin-rescue-end` block is used to handle exceptions.

```ruby
Ruby
begin
  # Code that might raise an exception
```

```ruby
  result = 10 / 0
rescue ZeroDivisionError => e
  puts "Error: #{e.message}"
end
```

Raising Exceptions

You can raise custom exceptions using the `raise` keyword:

```ruby
Ruby
def divide(a, b)
  if b == 0
    raise "Division by zero error"
  end
  a / b
end
```

Ensuring Code Reliability

Use `begin-rescue-end` blocks to handle potential exceptions gracefully.

Provide informative error messages to help with debugging.

Consider using `ensure` blocks to execute code regardless of whether an exception is raised.

Use `retry` to retry failed operations under certain conditions.

```ruby
Ruby
begin
  File.open("data.txt", "r") do |file|
    # Process the file
  end
rescue Errno::ENOENT => e
```

```
  puts "File not found: #{e.message}"
  retry  # Retry the operation
end
```

By effectively handling errors, you can create more robust and user-friendly Ruby programs.

6.2 Raising and Rescuing Exceptions in Ruby

Raising Exceptions

You can raise custom exceptions using the `raise` keyword. This allows you to signal specific error conditions and provide custom error messages.

```ruby
Ruby
def divide(a, b)
  if b == 0
    raise ZeroDivisionError, "Division by zero error"
  end
  a / b
end
```

Rescuing Exceptions

The `rescue` block in a `begin-rescue-end` block is used to catch and handle specific exceptions.

```ruby
Ruby
begin
  result = divide(10, 0)
rescue ZeroDivisionError => e
  puts "Error: #{e.message}"
end
```

Custom Exception Classes

You can define your own exception classes by subclassing the `StandardError` class.

Ruby
```ruby
class MyCustomError < StandardError
end

def my_method
  raise MyCustomError, "Something went wrong"
end
```

Ensuring Code Reliability

Use `begin-rescue-end` **blocks** to handle potential exceptions gracefully.

Provide informative error messages to help with debugging.

Consider using `ensure` **blocks** to execute code regardless of whether an exception is raised.

Use `retry` **to retry failed operations under certain conditions.**

Ruby
```ruby
begin
  File.open("data.txt", "r") do |file|
    # Process the file
  end
rescue Errno::ENOENT => e
  puts "File not found: #{e.message}"
  retry  # Retry the operation
end
```

By effectively raising and rescuing exceptions, you can create more robust and user-friendly Ruby programs.

6.3 Ensuring Code Reliability: Best Practices for Exception Handling

Effective exception handling is crucial for writing robust and reliable Ruby code. Here are some best practices to follow:

1. Use Specific Exception Classes

Raise specific exceptions to provide clear information about the error.

Use built-in exception classes like `StandardError`, `ArgumentError`, and `IOError` when appropriate.

Define custom exception classes for specific error conditions.

2. Handle Exceptions Gracefully

Use `begin-rescue-end` blocks to catch and handle exceptions.

Provide informative error messages to help with debugging.

Log errors to a log file or a monitoring service.

Consider using a centralized error reporting system.

3. Avoid Bare Rescues

Always specify the type of exception you want to catch.

Avoid using `rescue Exception` as it can mask underlying issues.

4. Use `ensure` Blocks

The `ensure` block guarantees that certain code will be executed, regardless of whether an exception is raised.

Use it to clean up resources like file handles or database connections.

5. Retry Failed Operations Judiciously

Use the `retry` keyword to retry failed operations under specific conditions.

Avoid excessive retries, as they can lead to infinite loops.

Implement a retry mechanism with exponential backoff to avoid overwhelming the system.

6. Test Your Exception Handling

Write unit tests to verify that your code handles exceptions correctly.

Simulate different error conditions to ensure your code behaves as expected.

Example:

```ruby
Ruby
def divide(a, b)
  if b == 0
    raise ZeroDivisionError, "Division by zero"
  end
  a / b
```

```ruby
end

begin
  result = divide(10, 0)
rescue ZeroDivisionError => e
  puts "Error: #{e.message}"
ensure
  puts "This code will always execute."
end
```

By following these best practices, you can write more reliable and maintainable Ruby code.

Chapter 7

Metaprogramming

7.1 Method Definition and Modification in Ruby

Method Definition

We've already seen how to define methods using the `def` keyword. However, Ruby offers more flexibility in defining methods dynamically.

1. Method Definition Using `define_method`:

Ruby
```
class MyClass
 define_method(:greet) do
  puts "Hello, world!"
 end
end

obj = MyClass.new
obj.greet
```

2. Method Definition Using `class_eval`:

Ruby
```
class MyClass
 class_eval do
  def hello
   puts "Hello from class_eval"
  end
```

```
  end
end
```

Method Modification

Ruby allows you to modify existing methods at runtime using `define_method` and `instance_eval`.

1. Modifying an Existing Method:

```ruby
Ruby
class MyClass
  def greet
    puts "Hello"
  end

  def modify_greet
    define_method(:greet) do
      puts "Hello, world!"
    end
  end
end

obj = MyClass.new
obj.greet  # Output: Hello
obj.modify_greet
obj.greet  # Output: Hello, world!
```

2. Adding Methods to an Instance:

```ruby
Ruby
class MyClass
  def initialize
    @name = "Alice"
```

```ruby
    end
  end

obj = MyClass.new
obj.instance_eval do
  def full_name
    "#{@name} Smith"
  end
end

puts obj.full_name  # Output: Alice Smith
```

Cautionary Note

While dynamic method definition and modification offer powerful capabilities, it's important to use them judiciously. Overusing them can make code harder to understand and maintain.

Best Practices:

Use dynamic methods for specific use cases, such as metaprogramming or DSLs.

Avoid modifying core methods of standard Ruby classes.

Test your code thoroughly to ensure that dynamic methods behave as expected.

By understanding these techniques, you can create more flexible and expressive Ruby code.

7.2 Open Classes and Monkey Patching in Ruby

Open Classes

In Ruby, classes are open, meaning you can add methods to them even after they've been defined. This feature is known as **monkey patching**.

Ruby
```ruby
class String
  def reverse_words
    self.split.reverse.join(" ")
  end
end

puts "hello world".reverse_words # Output: world hello
```

Here, we've added a `reverse_words` method to the `String` class.

Cautions and Best Practices

While monkey patching is a powerful technique, it's important to use it judiciously. Misusing it can lead to unexpected behavior and make code harder to understand and maintain.

Avoid Monkey Patching Core Classes: Modifying core classes like `String`, `Array`, or `Hash` can have unintended consequences, especially when working with libraries or frameworks that rely on their default behavior.

Test Thoroughly: When monkey patching, ensure that your changes don't introduce bugs or conflicts with other parts of your code. Write thorough tests to verify the behavior of your patched methods.

Use Mixins for Targeted Behavior: If you need to add specific behavior to multiple unrelated classes, consider using mixins instead of monkey patching. Mixins provide a more organized and predictable way to extend class functionality.

Be Mindful of Side Effects: Monkey patching can have unintended side effects, especially when multiple libraries or frameworks modify the same core classes. Be aware of potential conflicts and test your code carefully.

By following these guidelines, you can effectively use monkey patching to extend the functionality of existing classes while maintaining code quality and readability.

7.3 Metaclasses and Singleton Classes in Ruby

Metaclasses

In Ruby, every class is an object. This means that classes themselves have a class, which is called a **metaclass**. Metaclasses provide a powerful mechanism for metaprogramming, allowing you to modify the behavior of classes at runtime.

Accessing a Metaclass:

```ruby
Ruby
class MyClass
end

metaclass = MyClass.class
puts metaclass  # Output: Class
```

Modifying a Class's Behavior:

```ruby
Ruby
class MyClass
end

def MyClass.class_method
  puts "This is a class method"
end

obj = MyClass.new
MyClass.class_method
```

Singleton Classes

A singleton class is a class that has only one instance. It's often used to add methods to specific objects without affecting the entire class.

Creating a Singleton Class:

```ruby
Ruby
obj = Object.new
class << obj
  def my_method
    puts "This is a singleton method"
```

```
  end
end

obj.my_method
```

Key Points:

Metaclasses allow you to modify the behavior of classes at runtime.

Singleton classes allow you to add methods to specific objects.

Use metaprogramming techniques with caution, as they can make code more complex to understand and maintain.

Consider using mixins or modules to share common behavior between classes.

By understanding metaclasses and singleton classes, you can unlock advanced metaprogramming techniques in Ruby. However, it's important to use these tools responsibly and only when necessary.

Chapter 8

Ruby Gems and Libraries

8.1 The RubyGems Ecosystem: Discovering and Installing Gems

The RubyGems ecosystem is a vast collection of reusable libraries and tools that can significantly enhance your Ruby development experience.

Discovering Gems

RubyGems.org: The official repository for Ruby gems. You can search for gems by keyword, category, or author.

Bundler: A dependency management tool that helps you manage and install gems for your projects.

Installing Gems

Using the `gem` command:

Bash
```
gem install gem_name
```

Using Bundler:

Create a Gemfile: In your project's root directory, create a file named `Gemfile` and specify the required gems:

Ruby

```
source 'https://rubygems.org'
```

```
gem 'rails', '~> 7.0'
gem 'rspec', '~> 4.0'
```
Install Gems: Run the following command in your terminal:
Bash
```
bundle install
```

Organizing Gems in a Gemfile

The `Gemfile` is a crucial part of Ruby project management. It specifies the gems your project depends on and their versions. This ensures that your project can be easily deployed and maintained.

Key Points:

Gem Groups: You can organize gems into groups based on their purpose (e.g., development, test, production).

Gem Versions: Specify exact versions, version ranges, or platform-specific versions.

Bundler's `bundle exec`: Use this command to ensure that your project's gems are used when running scripts or commands.

Best Practices for Using Gems

Choose Reliable Gems: Look for gems with a good reputation, active development, and a large user base.

Update Gems Regularly: Keep your gems up-to-date to benefit from bug fixes and security patches.

Understand Gem Dependencies: Be aware of the dependencies of the gems you're using, as they can impact your project's performance and compatibility.

Use a Version Control System: This helps you track changes to your Gemfile and manage dependencies effectively.

By leveraging the RubyGems ecosystem, you can significantly accelerate your development process and build more robust and feature-rich Ruby applications.

8.2 Creating Your Own Gems: Packaging and Sharing Your Code

Why Create a Gem?

Reusability: Package your code into a gem to use it in multiple projects.

Sharing: Share your code with the Ruby community.

Dependency Management: Use gems to manage dependencies in your projects.

Steps to Create a Gem:

Set Up Your Gem:

Create a new directory for your gem.

Create a `Gemfile` to specify dependencies.

Create a `Gemfile.lock` to lock dependencies.

Create a `lib` directory to store your Ruby code.

Define Your Gem:

Create a `lib/your_gem_name.rb` file.

Define classes, modules, and methods that you want to include in your gem.

Write a `gemspec` File:

Create a `your_gem_name.gemspec` file.

Specify gem metadata like name, version, summary, author, and dependencies.

Ruby

```ruby
Gem::Specification.new do |spec|
  spec.name         = "your_gem_name"
  spec.version      = "0.1.0"
  spec.authors      = ["Your Name"]
  spec.email        = "your_email@example.com"
  spec.summary      = "Summary of your gem"
  spec.description  = "Detailed description of your gem"
  spec.homepage     = "https://github.com/your_username/your_gem_name"
  spec.license      = "MIT"

  spec.files        = `git ls-files`.split("\n")
  spec.executables  = spec.files.grep(%r{^bin/}) { |f| File.basename(f) }
  spec.test_files   = spec.files.grep(%r{^(test|spec|features)/})
  spec.require_paths = ["lib"]

  spec.add_development_dependency "bundler", "~> 2.3"
  spec.add_development_dependency "rspec", "~> 3.0"
end
```

Build the Gem:

Run the following command in your terminal:

Bash

gem build your_gem_name.gemspe

Install the Gem Locally:

Run the following command:

Bash

gem install ./your_gem_name-0.1.0.ge

Publish the Gem to RubyGems.org:

Create a RubyGems account.

Register your gem: `gem push your_gem_name-0.1.0.gem`

Best Practices for Creating Gems:

Clear Documentation: Provide clear and concise documentation for your gem.

Well-Structured Code: Organize your code into modules and classes for better readability and maintainability.

Thorough Testing: Write comprehensive tests to ensure the quality of your gem.

Version Control: Use a version control system like Git to track changes to your gem.

Consider a License: Choose an appropriate license to specify the terms of use for your gem.

By following these steps and best practices, you can create high-quality Ruby gems that benefit the community and streamline your development workflow.

8.3 Leveraging Popular Gems: A Quick Guide

RubyGems offers a vast ecosystem of libraries that can streamline your development process and add powerful features to your applications. Here are a few popular gems and their common use cases:

Common Task Gems

pry: A powerful Ruby REPL that provides advanced debugging and introspection capabilities.

rspec: A popular testing framework for writing clear and concise tests.

factory_bot: A library for creating test data.

faker: A library for generating fake data like names, addresses, and phone numbers.

pry-byebug: Combines the power of Pry and Byebug for advanced debugging.

rubocop: A static code analyzer to enforce style guides and improve code quality.

Web Development Gems

Rails: A full-stack web framework that simplifies web application development.

Sinatra: A lightweight web framework for creating small, focused web applications.

rack: A modular web server interface and toolkit.

activerecord: An ORM (Object-Relational Mapper) for interacting with databases.

rails-html-sanitizer: A library for sanitizing HTML to prevent XSS attacks.

Data Processing and Analysis Gems

nokogiri: An HTML, XML, and SAX parser.

open-uri: A library for opening URLs and reading their contents.

csv: A library for reading and writing CSV files.

json: A library for working with JSON data.

d3_js: A JavaScript library for data visualization that can be integrated with Ruby.

How to Use Gems

Install the Gem:

Bash
```
gem install gem_name
```
Require the Gem in Your Code:
Ruby
```
require 'gem_name'
```

Use the Gem's Features: Refer to the gem's documentation for specific usage instructions.

Example: Using the `pry` gem for debugging:

Ruby
```
require 'pry'
```

```
def my_method
  binding.pry
  # Code that might need debugging
end
```

Tips for Effective Gem Usage:

Choose the Right Gems: Select gems that align with your project's requirements and avoid unnecessary dependencies.

Keep Gems Updated: Regularly update your gems to benefit from bug fixes and security patches.

Understand Gem Dependencies: Be aware of the dependencies of the gems you use to avoid conflicts.

Write Clean and Well-Documented Code: Even when using powerful gems, write clear and maintainable code.

By effectively leveraging the RubyGems ecosystem, you can significantly boost your productivity and create more robust and feature-rich Ruby applications.

Chapter 9

Web Development with Ruby on Rails

9.1 Introduction to Rails: A Rapid Web Application Framework

Ruby on Rails, often abbreviated as Rails, is a powerful and flexible web application framework that allows developers to build complex web applications quickly and efficiently. It follows the Model-View-Controller (MVC) architectural pattern, which separates the application into three interconnected[1] parts:

Model-View-Controller (MVC) Architecture

Model: Represents the data and business logic of the application.

View: Handles the presentation layer, responsible for generating the user interface.

Controller: Manages the flow of the application, handling user requests and interacting with the model and view.

Key Features of Rails

Convention Over Configuration: Rails follows a set of conventions, reducing the need for extensive configuration.

Scaffolding: Generate basic application structures and boilerplate code quickly.

Active Record: Powerful ORM for interacting with databases.

Action Pack: Handles routing, controllers, and views.

Action Mailer: Provides easy-to-use email functionality.

Active Support: A collection of utility classes and modules.

Getting Started with Rails

Install Rails: Ensure you have Ruby and RubyGems installed. Then, install Rails using the following command:

Bash

```
gem install rails
```

Create a New Rails Application:
Bash
```
rails new my_a
```

Start the Development Server:
Bash
```
cd my_app
rails server
```

This will start a local development server, usually on port 3000.

Basic Rails Structure

A typical Rails application has the following directory structure:

```
my_app/
  app/
    controllers/
    helpers/
    models/
    views/
  config/
  db/
```

lib/
log/
public/
test/
vendor/
Gemfile
Gemfile.lock
config.ru
Rakefile

Building a Basic Rails Application

Generate a Model:

Bash

rails generate model Post title:string body:text

Generate a Controller:
Bash
rails generate controller Posts
Define Routes: Edit `config/routes.rb` to define routes:
Ruby
Rails.application.routes.draw do
  resources :posts
en
Create Views: Create views in `app/views/posts` to define how the posts will be displayed.

Implement Controller Actions: Implement actions in the `PostsController` to handle requests and interact with the `Post` model.

Further Exploration

Rails Guides: Official Rails documentation provides in-depth tutorials and guides.

Online Resources: Numerous online tutorials, courses, and communities offer support and learning resources.

Practice and Experiment: Build small projects to gain hands-on experience.

By leveraging Rails' powerful features and conventions, you can rapidly develop robust and scalable web applications.

9.2 Model-View-Controller (MVC) Architecture in Rails

The Model-View-Controller (MVC) architectural pattern is a fundamental design principle used in Rails to organize and structure web applications. It divides the application into three interconnected parts:

Model

The Model layer represents the data and business logic of the application. It typically interacts with the database to store and retrieve information.

Responsibilities:

Defines the data structure of the application.

Handles data validation and business rules.

Interacts with the database.

Example: A `Post` model might have attributes like `title`, `body`, and `created_at`. It could also have methods like `save`, `destroy`, and `comments`.

View

The View layer is responsible for presenting the user interface. It takes data from the controller and renders it into HTML, CSS, and JavaScript.

Responsibilities:

Displays information to the user.

Handles user input.

Renders HTML templates.

Example: A `posts/index.html.erb` view might display a list of posts, each with a title and a link to the post's details page.

Controller

The Controller layer acts as the intermediary between the Model and the View. It handles user requests, processes input, interacts with the Model, and selects the appropriate View to render.

Responsibilities:

Handles incoming requests from the user.

Processes the request and interacts with the Model.

Selects the appropriate View to render.

Redirects the user to different pages.

Example: A `PostsController` might have actions like `index`, `show`, `new`, `create`, `edit`, `update`, and `destroy` to handle different HTTP requests.

How They Interact

User Request: A user sends a request to the controller (e.g., by clicking a link or submitting a form).

Controller Processing: The controller receives the request and processes it. It may interact with the model to fetch or update data.

Model Interaction: The controller queries the model to retrieve or modify data from the database.

View Rendering: The controller selects the appropriate view and passes the necessary data to it.

Response to User: The view renders the HTML and sends it back to the user's browser.

By following the MVC pattern, Rails applications become more organized, maintainable, and scalable. It promotes code reusability, testability, and separation of concerns.

9.3 Building a Basic Rails Application: A Hands-on Tutorial

Setting Up Your Rails Environment

1. Install Ruby and Rails: Ensure you have Ruby and RubyGems installed. Then, install Rails using the following command:

Bash
gem install rails

2. Create a New Rails Application:

Bash
rails new my_app

This command will create a new directory named `my_app` with the basic Rails project structure.

Generating a Model

Let's create a simple blog application. We'll start by generating a `Post` model:

Bash
cd my_app
rails generate model Post title:string body:text

This command will create a `Post` model with `title` and `body` attributes. It will also create a migration file to update the database schema.

Running the Migration

To create the database tables, run the following command:

Bash
rails db:migrate

Generating a Controller

Next, let's generate a `PostsController` to handle requests related to posts:

Bash

```
rails generate controller Posts
```

This will create a `PostsController` with default actions like `index`, `show`, `new`, `edit`, `create`, `update`, and `destroy`.

Defining Routes

Edit the `config/routes.rb` file to define the routes for your application:

Ruby
```
Rails.application.routes.draw do
  resources :posts
end
```

Creating Views

Create views in the `app/views/posts` directory to define how posts will be displayed:

index.html.erb: Lists all posts.

show.html.erb: Displays details of a single post.

new.html.erb: Provides a form to create a new post.

edit.html.erb: Provides a form to edit an existing post.

Starting the Server

To start the development server, run the following command:

Bash
```
rails server
```

This will start a local server, usually on port 3000. You can access your application in your web browser by visiting `http://localhost:3000`.

Adding Functionality to the Controller

Edit the `PostsController` to define actions and handle requests:

```ruby
Ruby
class PostsController < ApplicationController
  def index
    @posts = Post.all
  end

  def show
    @post = Post.find(params[:id])
  end

  # ... other actions
end
```

Further Customization

Styling: Use CSS to style your application.

JavaScript: Use JavaScript to add dynamic behavior to your application.

Database Interactions: Use Active Record to interact with the database.

User Authentication: Implement user authentication and authorization.

Deployment: Deploy your application to a production server.

By following these steps and exploring the Rails documentation, you can build complex web applications with ease. Remember to experiment, learn from the community, and have fun!

Chapter 10

Advanced Ruby Topics

10.1 Concurrency and Parallelism in Ruby

Concurrency and parallelism are powerful techniques for improving the performance of your Ruby applications. Let's delve into these concepts and how to implement them in Ruby.

Concurrency vs. Parallelism

Concurrency: Multiple tasks execute concurrently, but not necessarily simultaneously. This can be achieved using threads, which share the same memory space.

Parallelism: Multiple tasks execute simultaneously on different CPU cores. This is typically achieved using processes, which have their own memory space.

Concurrency with Threads

Ruby provides a built-in Thread class to manage concurrent execution.

```
Ruby
Thread.new {
  puts "This is a new thread"
}.join
```

Key Points:

Shared Memory: Threads share the same memory space, which can lead to potential issues like race conditions if not handled carefully.

Global Interpreter Lock (GIL): Ruby's GIL limits the number of threads that can execute simultaneously on a single CPU core. While threads can improve responsiveness, they may not significantly improve performance for CPU-bound tasks.

Parallelism with Processes

For CPU-bound tasks, using processes can be more efficient. Ruby's `Process.fork` method can be used to create new processes.

```Ruby
fork do
  puts "This is a new process"
end
Process.waitall
```

Key Points:

Separate Memory Spaces: Processes have their own memory space, which avoids potential concurrency issues.

Inter-Process Communication (IPC): Processes can communicate using mechanisms like pipes, sockets, or shared memory.

Libraries for Concurrency and Parallelism

Concurrent Ruby: A comprehensive library for concurrent and parallel programming in Ruby.

Celluloid: An actor-based concurrency framework for building robust and scalable concurrent applications.

Best Practices

Understand the Problem: Identify tasks that can benefit from concurrency or parallelism.

Choose the Right Approach: Use threads for I/O-bound tasks and processes for CPU-bound tasks.

Manage Shared State Carefully: Use synchronization mechanisms like mutexes or semaphores to protect shared resources.

Test Thoroughly: Test your concurrent and parallel code to ensure correctness and avoid unexpected behavior.

Consider Asynchronous Programming: Use asynchronous programming techniques like event-driven programming or asynchronous I/O to improve performance without blocking the main thread.

By effectively utilizing concurrency and parallelism, you can write more efficient and responsive Ruby applications.

10.2 Functional Programming with Ruby

Functional programming is a programming paradigm that emphasizes the use of pure functions, immutability, and higher-order functions.[1] While Ruby is primarily an object-oriented language, it supports functional programming concepts.

Core Functional Programming Concepts in Ruby

Pure Functions:

A pure function always returns the same output for the same input.

It has no side effects, meaning it doesn't modify any external state.

Ruby
```
def add(a, b)
  a + b
end
```
Immutability:
Data should not be changed after it's created.

Ruby provides tools like `Object#freeze` to make objects immutable.

Ruby
```
array = [1, 2, 3]
frozen_array = array.freeze
```

Higher-Order Functions:

Functions that take other functions as arguments or return functions as results.

Ruby
```
def apply_function(function, argument)
  function.call(argument)
end

square = lambda { |x| x * x }
result = apply_function(square, 5)
```

Functional Programming Tools in Ruby

Blocks and Lambdas:

Blocks are anonymous functions that can be passed to methods.

Lambdas are objects that represent functions.

```ruby
Ruby
numbers = [1, 2, 3]
squares = numbers.map { |x| x * x }
```

Enumerable Module:
Provides methods like `map`, `reduce`, `filter`, and `each` for functional-style operations on collections.

```ruby
Ruby
numbers = [1, 2, 3, 4, 5]
even_numbers = numbers.select { |x| x.even? }
```

Benefits of Functional Programming

Readability: Functional code is often more concise and easier to understand.

Testability: Pure functions are easier to test, as they have no side effects.

Concurrency: Functional programming can help write concurrent and parallel code more safely.

Cautions and Considerations

Performance Overhead: Functional programming can sometimes be less efficient than imperative programming, especially when dealing with large datasets.

Learning Curve: Adopting a functional programming style may require a shift in thinking, especially for developers accustomed to imperative programming.

By understanding and applying functional programming concepts, you can write more elegant, maintainable, and efficient Ruby code.

10.3 Domain-Specific Languages (DSLs) with Ruby

A Domain-Specific Language (DSL) is a programming language tailored to a specific domain or problem. Ruby's metaprogramming capabilities make it an excellent language for creating DSLs.

Why Use DSLs?

Improved Readability: DSLs can make code more readable and concise for domain experts.

Reduced Complexity: DSLs can abstract away complex underlying implementations.

Increased Productivity: DSLs can automate repetitive tasks and streamline development.

Creating a DSL in Ruby

1. Define a Domain-Specific Syntax:

Use Ruby's syntax to create a language that resembles the domain's terminology.

Consider using keywords, symbols, or custom syntax to represent domain concepts.

2. Parse the DSL:

Use a parser generator like `Parslet` or a custom parser to analyze the DSL's syntax.

Convert the parsed syntax tree into a Ruby object.

3. Interpret or Compile the DSL:

Interpretation: Execute the DSL code directly, often using metaprogramming techniques.

Compilation: Translate the DSL code into another language (e.g., Ruby, C) for execution.

Example: A Simple SQL-like DSL

```ruby
Ruby
class Database
  def initialize(db_file)
    # ...
  end

  def query(sql)
```

```
   # Parse the SQL query and execute it
  end
end

db = Database.new("my_database.db")
db.query("SELECT * FROM users WHERE age > 18")
```

Metaprogramming Techniques for DSLs

Open Classes: Add methods to existing classes to extend their functionality.

Method Missing: Define a `method_missing` method to handle undefined methods.

Instance Eval: Execute code in the context of a specific object.

Popular DSL Frameworks in Ruby

Rake: A build tool that uses a DSL to define tasks and dependencies.

RSpec: A testing framework that uses a DSL to describe test cases.

Chef: A configuration management tool that uses a DSL to define system configurations.

Best Practices for Creating DSLs

Keep it Simple: Avoid overly complex syntax and semantics.

Prioritize Readability: Use clear and concise syntax.

Provide Good Error Messages: Help users understand and fix errors.

Test Thoroughly: Write comprehensive tests to ensure the correctness of your DSL.

Consider a Lexer and Parser: For more complex DSLs, a lexer and parser can help with syntax analysis.

By effectively leveraging Ruby's metaprogramming capabilities, you can create powerful and expressive DSLs tailored to specific domains, making your code more concise, readable, and maintainable.

www.ingramcontent.com/pod-product-compliance
Lightning Source LLC
Chambersburg PA
CBHW071010050326

40689CB00014B/3558